The Longan Tree

by Vo Tuan Hoang Vy

Mijikai Press

First published, 2011 as an ebook
Printed in the United States of America
First Printing, 2014
ISBN 0692234489

Mijikai Press
2901 Old Orchard Road
Raleigh, NC 27607

www.facebook.com/MijikaiPress

I give many thanks to Helen McCarthy for
encouraging my first English haiku, and
from the bottom of my heart, I would like
to thank Mr. Ed Bremson for many helps
he has given me.

Nothing left
But the colorful clouds
At the western sky
When the horizon just swallowed
The cake-shape sun.
~ Vo Tuan Hoang Vy

Introduction

I met Vo Tuan Hoang Vy, electronically, for the first time this summer on Twitter. He was the little guy from Vietnam, screen name @Vonguyenphong22, who posted all those delicately imaginative haiku day after day. I have a Masters degree in poetry, so I know a good poem when I see one, and I saw a lot of them from him as they magically scrolled down my computer screen. They were like beautiful flowers growing out of a terribly jumbled landscape. I messaged him that he should try to publish an ebook of his poems. When he investigated it, it all seemed too difficult, living in Vietnam as he does, being only 21, having no bank account, etc. I said I believed in him so much that I would publish the book for him. It has been a temptation for me to put Vy's poems into "good English." In some cases I have made certain corrections, but in some cases I have left the poems in his original version to preserve their natural poetic character and their unique vision. Anyway, I am now proud to present here Vo Tuan Hoang Vy's first collection of poems, 180 haiku, senryu and poetic images -- sweet like the longan fruit, often ethereal as the sky. They are sure to touch your imagination and your heart. Over and over I keep marveling at what a good young poet Vy is, and English is not even his native language. I'm impressed. Please buy a copy and enjoy. Sincerely, Ed Bremson, July 2011.

Please note: Each page contains a number of haiku, senryu, or tanka. Each poem is intended to be read individually, not in groups of two or three.

Fresh garden
Flooded with sunshine
Morning after rain.

A bird statue
Gazing at the sky
Dreams of flying.

Fluttering
On the road side
A tiny yellow flower.

Glistening
On the leaves
The last dewdrops.

Under the ancient bridge
A flow of water
An old color.

In the fresh air
Under the sunrise
Song of morrow.

Appearing in my hair
cherry-blossom petals
In a fairy dream.

On a lotus leaf
A green frog sitting
Singing a rain song.

A vermilion kiss
Of the sun
On the foliage.

Birdsong
Resounding in a blue dusk
Says goodbye to the sun.

The wind
Takes the cloud's hand
Leads it to heaven.

Tree by tree
Petal by petal
A rain of flowers.

Whose voice
Calling the violet petals
From the roadside?

Drop by drop
From the thatched roof
The rain singing.

From outside the window
Soft wind
Kisses my hair.

Under the old tree
A boy says some prayers
How is the future?

Roses
In the sunlight
Shining with their young color.

The sun
Kisses warmly on the hair
Of the foliages.

Here from my house
The birds sing a song
To welcome a new morning.

An old stone
Covered by green color
Silent under a tree.

Dark like night
Heavy like rock
A rain.

On the bird's wings
Snow-flakes
Black and white.

In the rain
Dancing
A red leaf.

Greening the earth
Light passes through the foliage
My cool feeling.

No one on the road
Just some wind and sun
And leaves falling.

The birds dreaming
Of a flying moment
Inside the eggs.

A dewdrop
Falling
From a lotus bud.

Under the bamboo grove
I hear the song
Of winds and leaves.

Leaning on the handrail
Of my memorial bridge
To hear the silent night.

I want to fly
With my own wings
Out of my heavy shoulders.

Bobbing on the waves
My paper boat
Dancing with the breeze.

The violins
Crickets playing
In darkness.

Near the pond
Green frogs singing
With the dark moon.

Picking up a wet curved leaf
Under a visionary moon
Cold air on my shoulder.

Darkness swallows the garden
And from within
A frog's lonely voice.

Dragonflies
Making a leaf
On a dead branch.

As the sun sets
Bamboos still singing
On this peaceful river bank.

Morning light
Passes through the pure water
The sun-washing carps.

A dead fly
One red dragonfly sitting
In the sad breeze of dusk.

Birdsong in the garden
The sun smiling
On tiny violet flowers.

The phantom's eyes
On the misty road
Wandering fireflies.

Just like a promise
The fireflies
Always around the graves.

Fireflies
Lighting up the river bank
Misty night.

Late bees
On the fully blossoming tree
Mottled dusk light.

The sleepy sun
Reflecting on the lake
And some carps.

Cicadas stop singing
As they cry
For the dead winds.

A violet flower
Lonely
Amid the dark gray earth.

Along the river
Fireflies
Blinking on the dark path.

Caroling on the trees
Some invisible birds
In the gathering dusk.

Chrysanthemums
Yellow and white
Along the gravel path.

The tiny bees
Moving around
Some sweet flowers.

Swaying, falling
A white petal
On the rock yard.

A yellow butterfly
And green moss
Filling an old stone.

Some sun-drops
On the wet cold yard
Under the sparse foliages.

Whose shadow
Passes on the dim road
In the rain?

White roses
On an old grave
butterflies.

A tiny spider
Clinging to its web
In the wind.

Birdsongs near an empty nest
Who picks up
An ever lost yesterday?

Darkness of dawn.
The dead wind
On an empty hill.

A bird on a bird
Singing and silent
A life and a stone.

Willows
Near the glittering lake
Some red flowers.

The only living pine
On that deadly shore
A somber glimmer of hope.

Singing with the rain
On the tree
A wet bird.

Nothing in the rain
Only a wet sparrow
On a fading branch.

Morning light
Glitters on the pond
When the winds pass by.

One flies and one sings
Two birds are thinking
Of a warm nesting.

After dark
Silence
Of my dreamy woods.

Falling out there
Some more raindrops
Sounding blue.

Sitting on a rose
A dragonfly
Boasting its blue color.

My paper boat
Moving on the pond
Turning in the wind.

It rains
On the lotus leaves
And the carps hear it.

A pink rose petal
Falling on a gray stone
Time to rest.

*next*Under water lilies
Hiding
Carps, red and white.

Whose voice
From the balcony?
Or just wind's sound
Passing by the clusters
Of blue roses.

After the squall
Night seems so sad
Some trees uprooted.

A blue dragonfly
Sitting on a leaf
In the drizzling rain.

A blue butterfly
On the pink flowers
The noon garden.

The scars
Of the fairy moon
Dark lights.

On the old pond
Together shining
Moon and fireflies.

Last night
On a willow branch
A hanging moon.

Half red moon
Appears from the east
Paper moon.

The lake willows
Cover the moon
Some leaking lights.

Water-lily flowers
Deep rouge color
Night fragrance.

Night moths
Talking with the lamp
Some last moments.

Morning river
Slowly glittering
Dancing waves.

Yesterday a broken branch
Hanging on the tree
Sighing for a fading life.

Some blossoms fall
As early winds flutter
Through the longan tree.

Fallen stars
There on the sea
Sparkling moments.

Quivering green grass
Covering the graves
Night breezes.

A lonely leaf
Sighs for its tree
As it slowly falls.

Dusk song
Of breezes and birds
Sinking my soul into darkness.

In the gray air.
Rain
On the mossy rock

Heating sunlight
On the windy shore
Blue and white.

Cicada's song
On the summer pavement
From yesterday.

Water dances out there
As winds roam
Together with rain.

An ancient branch
The crows sitting
Dusk enjoying.

Darkness
Falling on the lawn
Some cricket's sounds.

The fingers
Of the coconut leaves
Typing within the winds.

My purple dream
A cherry-blossom petal
Falling on the moon.

Dark air
A silent frog
Jumps onto a lotus leaf.

Orange color
On the banana leaves
Setting sun light.

The shadows
Dancing on the glass window
Western bamboo grove.

Yellow bees
Flying around
The longan trees.

Tiny boats
On the pond
Lotus petals.

On the noon lake surface
Some up and down dragonflies
Tiny waves.

Into my hand
From the mossy roof
Falls the last autumn leaf.

Breezes stir the air
And the leaves
Dancing on the roof.

On a sandy yard
Sun washing
A silky feather crow.

Humid air outside
I find a window
To hear birdsong.

Green moss
Covering the gray earth
An ancient footprint.

Swaying in the dusk light
Tiny and white
Longan flowers.

The sound of leaves
Drives me to sleep
Song on the coconut trees.

Sunlight on the roadside
The fallen violet petals
Of an unknown flower.

The old benches
On an ancient yard
The dust of time.

Hanging the moon
On the night branches
Careful! The lake's nearby.

On a spider web
Glistening in the moonlight
Dewdrops.

Ending its life
In a bright heaven
Moth around the lamp.

The crickets
Playing their violin concerto
Shining moon.

A silent shadow
On the broken wall
Who stands there?

Darkness of the trees
I see the shadows
Growing within the moonlight.

A full moon
In my honey cup
Drinking honey moon.

Touching the moon
And the waves appear
My silent pond.

Who misses fireflies
On this bright night
No more green light?

Missing the moon
Those happy carps
Swimming around the bright sphere.

Moonlight
Through sleeping leaves
Shadows of the night.

In the fading air
Dusk light
On waving coconut leaves.

On the glittering lake
Some colorful petals
Light of setting sun.

Sound of water
A broken branch
A leaving owl.

Throwing out the moon
From my cup of tea
Oh! Who hung you there?

Nothing left for the shining life
A dead firefly
Under a curved leaf.

A fanciful moon
On the silent lake surface
A reaching carp.

My dreamy moon
Out there on the faded branch
My reaching hand.

Moon dust
On my shoulder
Some hooting owls.

An old mossy road
My hesitant steps
Gray and green.

The glittering clouds
The sun hides behind
Some bird's shadows.

On the sunny road
Two quivering flowers
Showing their violet color.

On the fruiting longans
Singing the late summer song
Some late cicadas.

A night frog
Jumping on the moon
Water waves.

Fragrance of roses
Spreading in the cold air
Night moths.

Dark is blue
Light is ghost
Wind is song.

Night garden
Fireflies roaming
Phantoms smiling.

Blue is when
The moon's making tears
On its fairy light.

Wandering on the night shore
Winds take my hand
I feel the waves.

A flying lantern
Roaming on the starry sky
Two moons this night.

Fireflies glitter
On the dark mirror
Of the lake.

Stark air
Of the dusk rain
Beside my warm cat.

Midnight's sunshine
On the silent sky
A lone firefly.

Tiny rose
In her silent garden
Butterfly's dream.

Dancing raindrops
On the pond's surface
The summer sound.

Noontime
Sounds of cicadas
From the blossoming tamarind.

Shady path
Noon walking
Rain of yellow leaves.

White water-lily
The pure fragrance
Spreading in the air.

Splash of rain
On the brimming gutter
Ending the nap.

A wet frog
Sitting on a lotus leaf
Rain watching.

An old spider web
On the green branches
And breezes by the lake.

Blue color
Of the moonlight
On my fading hand.

Who kisses me
From my blind dream
Breezes sing on the sky.

The last moment
Of my far away dream
Sakura petals on my hair.

Moonlight
On the water-fall
A huge bright lantern.

Violet daisies
A sad color
On the flower pot.

Fairy sunset
The sun dying the sky
Into pure rouge.

Morning sunlight
Brightens the clouds
A white dragon appears.

Some red petals floating
On the lake surface
Breezes.

Dancing
With moonlight
Those fireflies.

Who hung the sun
On a slight bamboo
Falling down.

Whose shadow
Sitting there
On the waning moon?

The violet sunset
Calling the night
From its own tears.

Behind the rails
Of my summer window
I feel the dusk light.

Who made your tears
The sad gray statue
Garden after rain?

The ghosts of the past
Flying around the dark
The dust of time.

Rain sings on the roof
Sound of emptiness
Summer air.

Dust rain
In the glistening garden
Some fireflies.

The melody
Of the dusk breezes
Filling the air.

The dust from the stars
Falling into the pond
Glittering.

The phantom's eyes
On the misty road
Wandering fireflies.

Fireflies
Dancing on the starry pond
A lonely beauty.

Withering white
The owls sitting
Under the quarter moon.

Falling stars
On the glittering sky
Fairy night.

A dead branch
One red dragonfly sitting
In the sad dusk breeze.

Vo Tuan Hoang Vy, also known on Twitter as @vonguyenphong22, is now a twenty-four year old Vietnamese young man, who earned his undergraduate degree in Business Administration from Tien Giang University. This is his first published work.

Ed Bremson, who edited this book, is a published poet and retired State employee who lives in Raleigh, North Carolina. Ed (@EdBremson) met Vo Tuan Hoang Vy on Twitter in the summer, 2011.

Acknowledgements

The cover photo of Longan Tree fruit is a public domain photo from Wikipedia.

www.ingramcontent.com/pod-product-compliance
Lightning Source LLC
Chambersburg PA
CBHW051046030426
42339CB00006B/217